NORTH KOREA'S STRATEGIC INTENTIONS

North Korea is probably the most mysterious and inaccessible country in the world today. Officially known as the Democratic People's Republic of Korea (DPRK), the Pyongyang regime is headed by perhaps the most mercurial and enigmatic political leader alive. No prominent figure of the early 21st century has been more reviled by Americans or considered more dangerous to the United States—with the possible exception of Saddam Hussein and Osama Bin Laden—than Kim Jong Il.[1] The regime Kim leads is generally considered to be one of the most repressive in existence, with a vast gulag, a massive security apparatus, and an extensive system of controls. Despite the facade of a powerful party-state possessing an enormous military, the North Korean economy is in shambles, hundreds of thousands of its people are living either as refugees in China or as displaced persons inside their own country, and as many as three and a half million people have died from starvation and related diseases.[2]

Pyongyang is one of only two surviving members of the exclusive Axis of Evil club identified by President George W. Bush in January 2002. Topping the U.S. list of concerns about North Korea is its nuclear program—Washington is extremely alarmed not only that Pyongyang is developing a nuclear capability for its own use, but also proliferating nuclear material and technology. But the United States and other countries are also concerned about other weapons of mass destruction (WMD) that North Korea possesses, as well as its ballistic missile program. Moreover, North Korea's conventional military forces are sizeable with significant capabilities and confront the armed forces of the Republic of Korea (ROK) and the United States across the Demilitarized Zone (DMZ).

APPROACH

This monograph analyzes the North Korean regime's strategic intentions and motivations. I use the term "North Korean regime" to refer to the highest echelon of the power structure in Pyongyang—Kim Jong Il and his senior associates.[3] Subsequent monographs will examine North Korea's political and economic systems, its foreign relations, and its conventional military and WMD capabilities.

To begin, I survey and examine the views of six leading analysts of North Korea regarding Pyongyang's strategic intentions.[4] I have selected these analysts (in one case a two-person team)—Stephen Bradner, Victor Cha, Bruce Cumings, Selig Harrison, Kongdan Oh and Ralph Hassig, and David Kang—based on their significant records of substantial research and major publications on North Korean security issues and/or distinguished professional careers focused on North Korean security affairs.[5] Moreover, I have identified the six because they represent the wide spectrum of thinking about Pyongyang—indeed the assumptions and findings of these analysts vary considerably.

Analysts often are labeled in ideological terms as "liberal" or "conservative" in their views on North Korea. This is a legitimate distinction because it is important to recognize the possible biases experts may bring to their analyses and blinders they might have. However, such differentiation is of limited utility because some significant and surprising overlaps and commonalities exist, as well as contrasts in analyses of Pyongyang and policy prescriptions for Washington that do not seem to fit neatly into either a "left" or "right" position. For example, most analysts contend that North Korea is fearful of U.S. military capabilities, and most agree that Pyongyang is a morally repugnant and highly repressive totalitarian dictatorship.[6] Meanwhile they differ on the significance of ideology to North Korea—whether it makes Pyongyang more rigid or flexible in policymaking and decisionmaking. Some, such as Stephen Bradner, argue that North Korea's leaders are trapped in a kind of ideological straightjacket that tends to preclude certain policy options. Others assume that a significant number of North Korea's leaders are actually pragmatists, and the key barrier to major policy changes lies with the dogmatism of some entrenched "ideologues" in the elite.[7]

I use the terms "hardline" and "softline" broadly to classify an analyst's assessment of North Korean strategic intentions. But even within the hardline and softline "camps," one can find a diversity of assessments. This diversity can prove valuable in discerning the main points of controversy and identifying key common themes in

strategic assessments of North Korea. Furthermore, this approach will identify the fundamental assumptions that each analyst makes in his/her treatment of North Korea.

THE SPECTRUM OF EXPERT VIEWS OF NORTH KOREA'S INTENTIONS

Perhaps the most significant difference among the six analysts is in their assessments of the likelihood that the regime will moderate its policies. By moderate, I mean pursue economic reforms, reduce defense spending, and improve relations with perceived adversaries, notably the United States. Assessments range from a belief that Pyongyang is already in the process of moderating at one extreme to the belief that Pyongyang will never moderate at the other. The key variable is motivation—what drives the regime? Motivation, however, is a difficult dimension to identify and gauge.

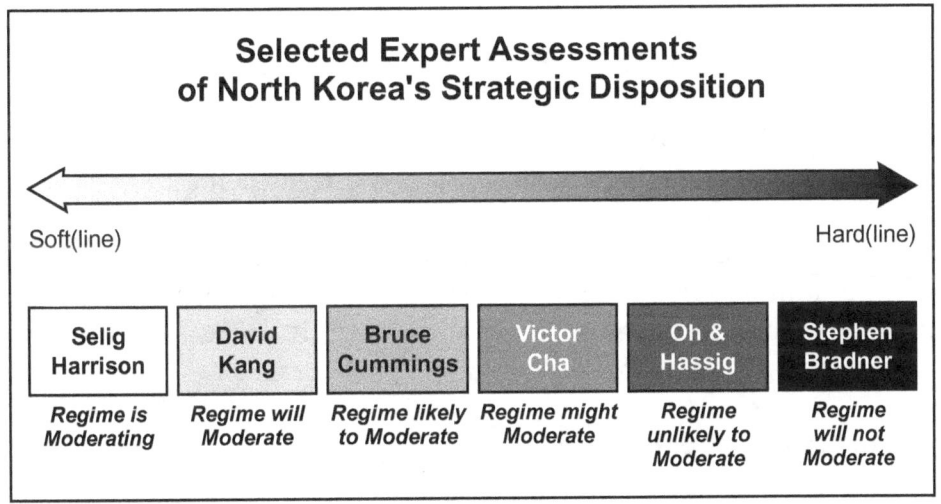

Figure 1.

Selig Harrison: *Regime Is Moderating.*

Selig Harrison is a long time observer and writer on the subject of North Korea who has visited the country at least six times (1972, 1987, 1992, 1994, 1996, and 2005). Of the six analysts under review, he is the most benign in his assessment of North Korean intentions. He argues that a "fundamental change in the North Korean worldview during the past three decades" has occurred. While Harrison admits that Pyongyang continues to possess a "siege mentality," he nevertheless asserts the regime has undertaken a "steady liberalization of economic life." He contends that Kim Jong Il is pursuing "reform by stealth" because the pace and scope of economic change depends on a struggle between an "Old Guard" faction and "reformers" in the North Korean leadership.[8]

Harrison argues it is crucial that the United States support the reformers by pursuing more accomodationist policies toward North Korea. Since Pyongyang has a heightened threat sensitivity to Washington, if the United States moderates its approach, this will strengthen the hands of the moderates and hence provide greater impetus for further reform and opening. North Korea, in Harrison's view, has also sought arms control agreements and has periodically made proposals for troop reductions.[9]

Harrison asserts that it is very difficult for North Korea's leaders to renounce publicly the goal of full Korean unification because this is a key legitimacy issue for the Pyongyang regime.[10] He argues that North Korea's leaders are actually seeking confederation between the two Koreas, and this has been a consistent theme put forward by Pyongyang since 1972. Harrison contends that North Korea is fearful of the United States, and this is the reason for building a large military. Pyongyang, he claims, only developed its nuclear program when a "severe deterioration" in the "military readiness" of its conventional forces occurred.[11]

David Kang: *Regime Will Moderate*.

David Kang, a scholar at Dartmouth College, specializes in North Korean security issues. He argues that Pyongyang has tenaciously gone about ensuring "regime survival" the most logical way a small, weak and vulnerable state can—by winning a reputation for acting in a dangerous and unpredictable manner—a strategy Kang dubs "deterrence through danger."[12] Kang stresses that the reason North Korea is so highly militarized and has pursued a nuclear program is because it believes it is facing a massive security threat

from overwhelming U.S. might. The purpose of its sizeable military machine is "deterrence and defense" against the United States.[13] Kang insists that the regime wants to moderate and will do so under the proper conditions. These conditions are predicated on the United States taking a less hostile and threatening approach to North Korea.[14]

Kang argues that for 4 decades following the Korean War, North Korea remained in a "holding pattern" with "minor changes" in foreign policy and no reform.[15] But in recent years the regime has pursued a "cautious and tentative" opening in economic and diplomatic spheres.[16] If the perceived threat from the United States diminishes, then Pyongyang will more vigorously pursue economic reforms. Kang argues that it is "highly unlikely that North Korea currently retains such aggressive intentions [i.e., plans to invade South Korea] in any serious way."[17]

Bruce Cumings: *Regime Likely to Moderate.*

Bruce Cummings is the most renowned historian of modern Korea, and his prolific publications include a two-volume history on the origins of the Korean War. While he is routinely considered pro-Pyongyang in his views, this characterization is inaccurate. Although Cumings does tend to be somewhat sympathetic to North Korea, he is certainly no apologist for the regime. Indeed, Cumings is clear-eyed about the horrors of the system, openly critical of it, and not sanguine in his assessments of the current situation. He contends that Pyongyang is "neither muddling through . . . nor is it seriously reforming like China and Vietnam." He laments that, during the past decade, the system was beset by "paralysis and immobilism."[18] North Korea, he says, is "the most astounding garrison state in the world" and "deeply insecure, threatened by the world around it." Precisely because of this insecurity, Cumings—like David Kang—argues that the regime "projects a fearsome image."[19] Nevertheless, he seems to believe that the regime would likely moderate if the United States eased its hawkish approach. Cumings appears to suggest that Pyongyang has given up on unification and desires "peaceful coexistence with the South."[20]

Victor Cha: *Regime Might Moderate.*

Victor Cha, a professor at Georgetown University until he joined the staff of the National Security Council in late 2004, is a leading scholar of contemporary East Asian security. In recent years, he has focused on North Korea and tends to be viewed as hawkish. Indeed, he has advocated a policy approach for the United States dubbed "hawk engagement." In fact, he is less harsh than his reputation would lead one to believe.

Cha argues, while the United States must be tough on North Korea, that does not mean Washington should refuse to engage Pyongyang. He contends that North Korea feels threatened by the United States. Cha suggests it is possible that North Korea might be willing to moderate, and the United States should pursue this possibility but with caution and willingness to employ a stick when necessary. He does believe that Pyongyang has given up on unification on its terms, and hence it is conceivable that the regime might be willing to moderate its policies.

Nevertheless, while North Korea has lowered its expectations, Cha believes that "Pyongyang's endgame . . . [now boils down] to basic survival, avoiding collapse, and avoiding domination by Seoul."[21] North Korea's leadership recognizes that it is weaker than South Korea and has concluded that time is not on its side. Cha fears that Pyongyang "could perceive some use of limited force as a rational and optimal choice, even when there is little or no hope of victory."[22] He dubs this concern "lashing out." In short, Cha worries that North Korea might be getting more desperate and hence more prone to act violently.

Kongdan Oh/Ralph Hassig: *Regime Unlikely to Moderate.*

Kongdan Oh and Ralph Hassig are long-time analysts of North Korea—Oh is a researcher at the Institute for Defense Analyses, and Hassig is a professor of psychology. They believe that the regime is unlikely to moderate because this will likely undermine its position. Most, if not all, measures adopted during the past few years which have been characterized as reforms actually appear to be ad hoc adjustments (or "modifications") to ensure the survivability of the regime rather than part of any thoroughgoing reform effort.[23] Moreover, Pyongyang almost certainly will not agree to give up completely its nuclear program or negotiate away other WMD or missile programs because "military strength" is seen as vital to ensuring the survival of the regime.[24] The regime, Oh and Hassig argue, has not given up on attaining unification on its terms and, under certain circumstances, could possibly launch an attack across the DMZ.[25]

Stephen Bradner: *Regime Will Not Moderate.*

Stephen Bradner is a veteran analyst of North Korean security affairs who has served for many years as special advisor to the Commander of U.S. Forces in Korea. The most hawkish of the analysts reviewed here, he argues that the likelihood of North Korea moderating is virtually nil. Bradner asserts that Pyongyang is tightly and brutally controlled by one kinship group—what he calls the Kim Family Regime. This regime is single-minded in its determination to unify the Korea Peninsula on its own terms.

Despite the severe economic difficulties North Korea has faced over the past decade and a half, Bradner contends that the regime has not scaled back its goals nor curbed its ambitious plans. Pyongyang is focused single-mindedly on maintaining a powerful military to the detriment of all else ("maximizing its military power").[26] North Korea's leaders will never give up their WMD or missile programs.[27] "They will not reform," although the regime "may cautiously hazard some limited experimentation."[28] Instead Pyongyang's leaders will likely continue to pursue an "aid-based strategy" of accepting or extorting handouts from foreign governments and nongovernment organizations (NGOs), pending the achievement of their ultimate goal.[29] North Korea's leadership believes the road to its unification goal leads through military preparedness and defeating the enemy.

According to Bradner, Pyongyang recognizes that the troops of the United States and ROK Combined Forces Command constitute a formidable and determined foe. Its strategy is to weaken its adversary through undermining and eventually breaking the alliance.[30] The goal is to bring about the withdrawal from South Korea of U.S.

forces. Since Pyongyang views Seoul as a puppet regime that cannot stand without U.S. backing, once this withdrawal has occurred, North Korea believes the South will be ripe for the taking. Bradner argues that Pyongyang "will not reconcile with the South" but rather is intent on overthrowing the Seoul government.[31]

Observations and Analysis.

All of the analysts surveyed concur on a number of conclusions. While they may seem basic and even obvious, they bear stipulating. First, each assumes that the North Korean regime is not irrational, and there is an internal logic to its words and deeds. Of course, the experts tend to differ on what this internal logic is. While there never cease to be those in the media who are eager to proclaim that North Korea's leaders are crazy, all serious observers of the Pyongyang regime tend to insist that, quite to the contrary, they can detect a perverse logic and clear pattern of behavior from North Korea. Cha and Kang assert North Korea is "neither irrational nor undeterrable."[32] Kang argues that Pyongyang deliberately depicts itself as dangerous to deter the enemy. Oh and Hassig also argue that North Korean leaders consciously have cultivated an image of irrationality to serve as a deterrent effect.[33] This is not to say that even veteran analysts have not at times betrayed a sense of frustration in seeking to make sense of the Pyongyang regime.[34]

Second, in the consensus view of assembled experts, this rationality leaves North Korea's leadership with a heightened sense of insecurity. While leaders of communist countries tend to be prone to paranoia in the first place, the Pyongyang regime also believes that it faces a very real threat from the armed forces of the United States and ROK. They appear truly afraid of possible attack. This fear may have heightened in the spring of 2003 when U.S. and coalition forces toppled the regime of Saddam Hussein in Iraq because North Korea feared that it might be the next object of an American military operation.[35]

At a minimum, the North Korean leadership probably believes that in any major force-on-force conflict with the United States the Korean People's Army would be defeated, leading to the collapse or overthrow of the regime. The clearest indication of this fear and the existence of this logic in the north is that, for more than half a century, Pyongyang has not launched an attack southward across the DMZ. In other words, the presence of U.S. Forces in Korea (USFK) immediately below the DMZ appears to have deterred North Korea. Pyongyang's leaders know that from the very start of any attack on South Korea, they would be battling U.S. military forces and be at war with the United States.[36] In short, deterrence seems to have worked.

Third, North Korea's rulers—or at least some of them—appear to be acutely aware of the dilemma they face. On the one hand, they seem to recognize that, on the surface of it, the most logical way to rescue their economy is to adopt thoroughgoing reforms. On the other, they seem to realize that pursuing such a course is likely to mean that they would be undermining their positions in the process—threatening their own power and control. Such reforms might be so successful that after gathering momentum, the regime would eventually find itself reformed out of existence. Because North Korea's leaders fear this would be the outcome, they are reluctant to move down what they view as the slippery slope of reform.[37] Of course, the alternative—to undertake little or no reform—is just as problematic. Without significant reform, North Korea's leaders realize they are probably condemning their regime to the ash heap of history. In short, they are damned if they do and damned if they don't. Pyongyang is probably more fearful of initiating change that it fears will spiral out of control than it is of doing little or nothing.

STRATEGIC INTENTIONS

After surveying the range of expert views about North Korean thinking, what can one now say about the strategic intentions of Pyongyang's leaders? In the absence of access to internal documents and interviews with key North Korean policymakers, one cannot say with certainty. Yet on the basis of the assessments of North Korea reviewed above, it seems prudent to narrow the range of possibilities to three alternatives for the thrust of North Korean strategic intentions: modest/security, ambitious/benevolent, or ambitious/malevolent (see Figure 2).

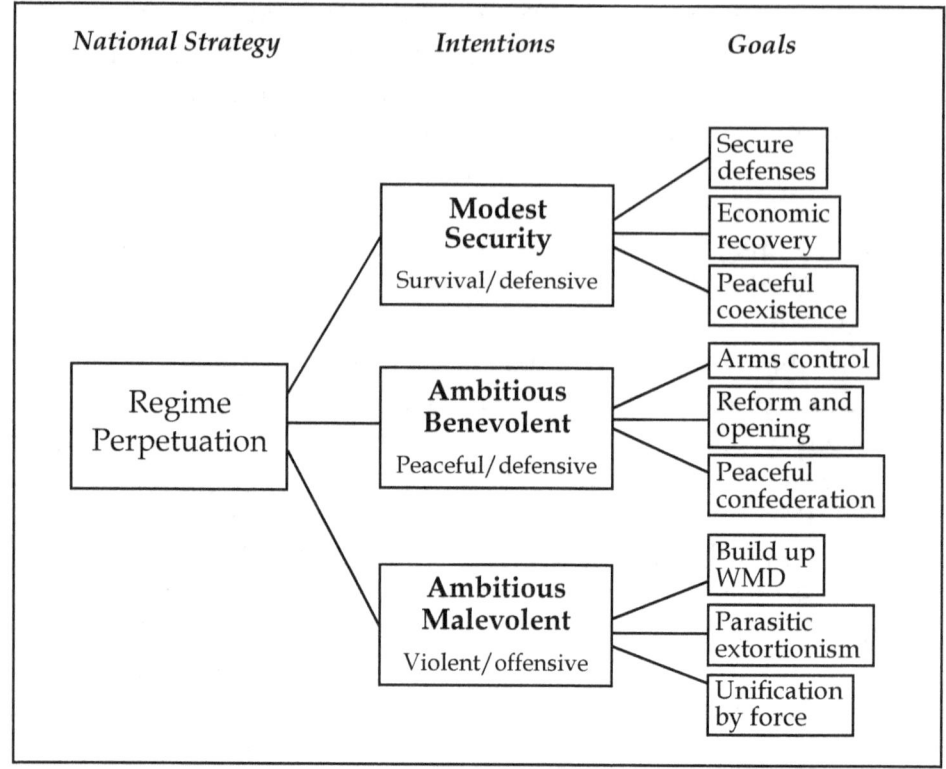

| National Strategy | Intentions | Goals |

Figure 2. Pyongyang's National Strategy, Intentions, Goals, Circa 2004-05.

Modest/Security.

The first possible set of Pyongyang's strategic intentions comes down to a single overriding modest aim: the survival of the North Korea regime. The paramount goal is to ensure that North Korea is adequately protected. Pyongyang would be willing to negotiate but reluctant to agree to give up its nuclear or missile programs. The siege mentality would be alleviated if North Korea could be reassured adequately that the United States and South Korea do not threaten it. Then it might be possible for Pyongyang to develop a more conciliatory relationship with Seoul—a policy of peaceful coexistence. Harrison, Kang, and Cumings believe Pyongyang subscribes to this set of intentions.

Ambitious/Benevolent.

The second package of intentions is a driving desire to maintain a strong, independent, and autonomous North Korea. Pyongyang would still need to conquer its siege mentality, but confidence-building measures might increase trust. This alternative would entail Pyongyang making peace with its long time adversaries in Seoul and Washington. North Korea would also desire to undertake thoroughgoing economic reforms and become an integral part of the global economic system. It would be prepared cautiously but purposefully to reduce—but probably not give up—its massive military through arms control efforts—conventional, WMD, missiles, and personnel—while seeking ways to guarantee North Korea's security. This represents an extremely ambitious but peaceful and defensive strategy. Harrison and Kang would certainly concur with most elements of this set of intentions, and Cumings, Cha, and Oh and Hassig would likely be prepared to entertain this possibility.

Ambitious/Malevolent.

The third possible set of North Korean strategic intentions is ambitious but extremely aggressive. In this option, Pyongyang has not given up on the conquest of South Korea through violence and/or deceit: unification on North Korea's terms. In this scenario, North Korean leaders would not be seeking merely to protect themselves and deter a possible attack by the United States and/or ROK. Rather, Pyongyang would desire to possess the conventional and unconventional capabilities to topple Seoul by force and deception. For this set of intentions, nuclear weapons and other WMD are essential offensive or at least coercive weapons, and North Korea will never give them up. Pyongyang would not see an urgent need to repair its deplorable economy, because it views the current priority as maintaining a military capable of attacking the forces of the United States and South Korea. In other words, North Korea has a wartime economy and rather than be diverted from its consuming focus of military preparedness, Pyongyang intends to sustain itself in the interim by extorting aid and revenue by whatever means necessary (including criminal activities). Bradner clearly believes this set of goals most accurately reflects North Korean intentions.

So, what are the intentions of the North Korean regime? Is it package #1, #2, or #3? Often analysts argue that Pyongyang's priority is simply "regime survival." As Bradner writes, "It has . . . become fashionable to describe North Korea's objective as survival."[38] But this probably does not capture its intent accurately. Kim Jong Il and his associates do not simply want to survive, they want to perpetuate and sustain their system. Fighting merely to survive would be implicitly to accept ultimate defeat, inevitable decline, and/or the DPRK's inferiority vis-à-vis the ROK. It is unlikely that North Korea's current leaders, at least the highest echelon, have lost all hope and have fatalistically accepted that the end of the DPRK looms on the horizon. But one must consider the possibility that this may be so. Cha argues this and outlines a worrisome mindset imbued with logic that might lead North Korea to "lash out" militarily to assure "basic survival."[39]

What all of the above analysts assume (rightly in my view) is that North Korea's rulers are rational. However, a tendency exists to succumb to the presumtion of clear-eyed and absolute rationality. Most analysts surveyed here have refrained from assuming perfect logic and recognize Pyongyang's leaders' reasoning is likely constrained or limited by the view from where they sit gazing out on the world. North Korea's rulers are influenced by history, ideology, and notions of nationalism that produce what social scientists term a "bounded rationality."[40] Nevertheless, some analysts appear to presume North Korea's leaders are capable of rationally calculating their options and in possession of a complete and accurate picture of the situation on the Korean peninsula. Cha and Kang, for example, fundamentally assume that Pyongyang's rulers have weighed all the statistics and, after comparing North and South Korea by the numbers, have determined that Seoul's system is superior. According to Cha and Kang, the only conclusion that Pyongyang can logically draw is that there is no conceivable way the regime can possibly emerge victorious under current conditions, and urgent action is needed. Cha argues that the regime is desperate and preoccupied with avoiding collapse and absorption by South

Korea.[41] Kang argues that "the flurry of North Korean diplomatic and economic activities in the past few years show that the North Korean leadership is actively pursuing a strategy they hope will ease their domestic problems." While Kang argues that there is "little evidence that North Korea is backed into a corner" and the regime has "not given up hope," Pyongyang, nevertheless, does appear to believe that urgent measures are necessary according to Kang.[42]

But what if North Korea's rulers do not have all the facts? And what, even if they have "all the facts" or at least most of them, they remain convinced of the superiority of their own system and confident in their ultimate victory? My own conclusion is that North Korea's senior leaders are determined and confident that they will not only survive, but that they will be able to restore and revitalize their regime. While most agree that they possess a siege mentality, they are not defeatists and retain a high degree of self-confidence, if not outright arrogance. Kim and other leaders are not crazy or irrational but they are almost certainly extremely ambitious. Kang argues "the North Korean leadership—far from having lost all hope and going into a bunker mentality—has been actively pursuing a number of options through which it can survive into the future."[43] Madeleine Albright remarked that when she met with Kim Jong Il in Pyongyang in November 2000, he "seemed confident"; he certainly "didn't seem a desperate or even worried man."[44] If this reasoning is correct, it rules out option #1. But beyond the likely strong desire to persevere and reenergize the DPRK, what can one say about North Korean intentions with a high degree of confidence? To address this question one needs to look closely at observable manifestations.

PROPAGANDA, POLICY, AND PLANNING

What are the observable manifestations that would indicate which of the three sets of strategic intentions North Korea is pursuing? There are three kinds of manifestations: (1) propaganda, (2) policy, and (3) planning. Each will be examined with regard to four areas: general intentions, security intentions, economic intentions, and intentions regarding unification.

Propaganda.

Propaganda is all pervasive—evident in virtually all official documents and public pronouncements. There are two aspects of propaganda: ideology and rhetoric. Ideology, or "basic principles," many analysts argue, is critical to understanding the North Korea regime.[45] First, we will examine what experts say about Pyongyang's ideology, and then we will look at the regime's own rhetoric.

Ideology. Officially, ideology remains central for Pyongyang, and hence some dogmatic justification or rationale must be forthcoming on virtually any issue. The key element of the ideology is the Cult of Kim Il Sung as manifest in the concept of *Juche* (also written *Chuch'e*). According to North Korean propaganda, citizens of the country owe everything to the "Great Leader." His brilliance and superhuman efforts have made the DPRK what it is today. And Kim Il Sung is credited with having "invented" *Juche* in the 1930s.[46] The ideology is portrayed as being uniquely Korean. In fact, the "idea of *chuch'e* is . . . firmly rooted in the experience of the North Korean people and Kim Il Sung."[47] The concept highlights the role of a supreme leader—*suryong*—and stresses the importance of unity and loyalty.[48]

Although *Juche* is normally translated as "self-reliance," it is perhaps more accurate to translate it as "Korea first." Putting Korea first is the opposite of accepting a subservient role for the country. In this sense, *Juche* can been seen as the opposite of tributary status. According to propaganda, North Korea today stands on its own proudly and bows to no one. It is no longer the supplicant to China it was in dynastic times. In a dramatic reversal, today dignitaries from other countries come to North Korea bearing gifts.

For *Juche* to be perpetuated, it must be continually validated in the eyes of North Korean people, which occurs in at least three ways. First, foreigners travel to Pyongyang. Most important are foreign leaders and dignitaries who come and pay their respects to Kim Il Sung by visiting his mausoleum. They also meet with other leaders, including Kim Jong Il. These visits are prominently shown on North Korean television and reported in the print media which depicts them as pilgrimages. Second, North Korea receives aid from abroad which is portrayed as tribute or gifts from around the world.[49] Both the flow of people and gifts are used by the regime to demonstrate that North Korea is a powerful and respected country. Of course there is a paradox: on the one hand, veneration and tribute from foreigners is seen as positive, but at the same time, *Juche* represents a "xenophobic nationalism" that teaches North Koreans to be wary and suspicious of foreigners.[50]

Third, for *Juche* to be validated, the regime must be seen to keep the country strong and continue to make at least token efforts toward unification. This requires staunch political "independence" (or *chaju*), "self-defense" (or *chawi*), and economic "self-sustenance" (or *charip*).[51] Kim Jong Il's primary theme has become *kangsongtaeguk*.[52] This slogan translates as "strong development, powerful country." How does the regime ensure a strong and powerful country? Unifying the peninsula would seem to be the strongest guarantee. How can the regime justify the continued sacrifices it asks of its citizens? These are rationalized as only temporary. The implicit logic is North Korea must maintain a strong military while enduring temporary economic hardships, pending unification of the Koreas. The stress on achieving "a unified, self-reliant, independent state free of foreign interference" is traceable back to pre-Korean War speeches given by Kim Il Sung.[53] Pyongyang believes that realization of unification will ensure a powerful independent country with a revitalized economy.

Rhetoric. Although the words in public pronouncements, official documents, and news releases are invariably propaganda, they can reflect actual thinking, reveal key trends, and indicate significant changes. While bluster, threat, and hyperbole are staples of North Korean documents and pronouncements, if examined methodically, they can provide insights or at least hints of regime intentions. These include the various versions of the DPRK's constitution, party documents, major editorials in the most prominent publications, and the text of public statements by senior officials. For the purposes of this analysis, I will limit my examination to four key items: the 1998 state constitution, the 2000 Inter-Korean summit news release, the five most recent New Year's editorials (2001-05) jointly published in the three leading newspapers (*Nodong Sinmun, Josoninmingun,* and *Chongnyonjonwi*), the statements made following each of the three rounds of Six Party Talks held in Beijing in 2003 and 2004 (April 23-25, 2003; August 27-29, 2003; and February 25-28, 2004), and the

Foreign Ministry statement of February 10, 2005. I consider four areas: the general situation, security, the economy, and unification.

General Situation. The current state constitution, amended in 1998, appears more Kim Il Sung-centric and nativist than earlier versions. First, this constitution contains a brand new preamble which is essentially a "eulogy" to the late North Korean leader.[54] Second, the post of state president was abolished, and deceased leader Kim Il Sung is designated "eternal president." There are no mentions of Marxism-Leninism, and only vague references to "socialism"—all overshadowed by constant harping on *Juche*. This is the guiding theoretical principle for North Korea and is attributed to the genius of Kim Il Sung.

According to Article 11 of the Constitution, "all activities" of the state should be conducted "under the leadership" of the Korean Workers' Party (KWP). Despite this assertion, repeated emphasis on the centrality of the armed forces, in such places as the highly authoritative annual New Year's joint editorials, call into question the leadership role of the KWP. The January 1, 2005, editorial, for example, urges the people to give "priority to military affairs" and "unite as one . . . [to] demonstrate the might of *Songun* [military first]!"[55] The editorial also insists: "The People's Army is the mainstay and main force of the *Songun* revolution." While this contrasts with an emphasis on a leading role for the "Party's leadership" in the January 2004 editorial, the 2005 editorial was consistent with the exhortations of the previous 2 years' editorials (2002 and 2003) to advance under the "Army-Based" banner.

Security. The defense portion of the 1998 amended constitution remains unchanged over the previous version. National defense continues to be the "supreme duty and honor of citizens. Citizens shall defend the country and serve in the army as required by law (article 86)." The January 2005 New Year's editorial exhorts the people to "actively learn from the People's Army's fighting spirit, work style and traits."

Both the January 1, 2005, editorial and February 10, 2005, Foreign Ministry statement insist that the United States should end its "hostile policy" towards North Korea.[56] The 2004 editorial also noted the "extremely hostile policy" of the United States. The editorial calls upon "All Koreans . . . [to] stage a powerful struggle . . . to drive the

U.S. troops out of south Korea [and thereby] remove the very source of a nuclear war." The January 2004 editorial pledged Pyongyang's commitment "to seek a negotiated peaceful solution to the nuclear issue between the DPRK and the U.S." This statement underscored the statement of a DPRK Foreign Ministry spokesman 4 months earlier on August 30, 2003, following the conclusion of the second round of the Six Party Talks. He said: "The DPRK made clear its consistent stand on the denuclearization of the Korean peninsula." The DPRK spokesman ridiculed the U.S. insistence on "complete, verifiable, and irreversible dismantlement" of Pyongyang's nuclear program. If Washington would only take positive steps to improve relations after North Korea had disarmed:

> This means that the U.S. is asking the DPRK to drop its gun first, saying it would not open fire, when both side[s] are leveling guns at each other. How can the DPRK trust the U.S. and drop its gun? Even a child would not be taken in by such a trick. What we want is for both side[s] to drop guns at the same time and co-exist peacefully.

The spokesman then went on to state that as a result of the U.S. position, Pyongyang had concluded: "that there is no other option for us but to further increase the nuclear deterrent force as a self-defensive measure to protect our sovereignty." The same February 10, 2005, Foreign Ministry statement announcing an "indefinite" suspension of North Korea's participation in the Six Party Talks also declared that Pyongyang possessed "manufactured nuclear weapons." The statement concluded by insisting that North Korea, nevertheless, remained committed to "the ultimate goal of denuclearizing the Korean Peninsula."

The 2003 and 2002 New Year's editorials were somewhat more strident, emphasizing North Korea's "military-based policy" and echoing the language of the 2001 New Year's editorial. The January 2001 joint editorial was very clear: "The policy of giving priority to the army is the permanent strategic objective in the present-time." The 2004 editorial notes that the SPA "strengthened" the political system by enhancing the "exceptionally high . . . authority" of the National Defense Commission "to meet the requirements of the *Songun* era."

Economy. According to article 34 in the DPRK Constitution, the "national economy of the DPRK is a planned economy." In terms of planning, the top priority continues to be national defense, and therefore it is no surprise that the 2005 editorial insists that "The defense industry is the foundation of the nation's military and economic potentials." The editorial states emphatically: "It is imperative to supply everything necessary for the defense industry on a preferential basis, pursuant to the Party's line of economic construction in the Songun era."

Despite the emphasis on national defense, the civilian sector does get attention in the constitution as well as in each New Year's editorial over the past 5 years. Article 37 of the amended constitution of 1998 includes the following new sentence: "The state shall encourage institutions, enterprises, or associations of the DPRK to establish and operate equity and contractual joint venture enterprises with corporations or individuals of foreign countries within a special economic zone." Furthermore a new phrase is inserted in article 33: "The state shall introduce a cost accounting system in the economic management . . . and utilize such economic levers as prime costs, prices, and profits." The 2003, 2004 and 2005 New Year's editorials all stress the necessity of improving "economic management." The 2003 editorial states: "We should manage and operate the economy in such a way as to ensure the largest profitability while firmly adhering to . . . socialist principles."

Regularly singled out in January 1 editorials as "the most important front[s] in socialist economic reconstruction" (2001 editorial) or as "a main link on efforts to revitalize the national economy" (2003 editorial) are: "power, coal mining, metal industries, and railway transportation." In January 2005, however, agriculture was declared "the main front of socialist economic construction." Increased attention to consumer goods is also stressed (2004 and 2005 editorials). Efforts are also urged to increase energy output and push forward with modern "science and technology" (2002, 2003, 2004, and 2005 editorials).

Unification. Unification figures prominently in all of the items under review. The preface to the current DPRK constitution states: "Kim Il Sung set reunification of the country as the nation's supreme task. . . ." And reunification is mentioned five times in the preface.

But the most prominent item is the "North-South Joint Declaration" issued by ROK President Kim Dae Jung and Kim Jong Il on June 15, 2000, at the conclusion of their summit in Pyongyang. The document highlights the common aspiration of both Pyongyang and Seoul as "peaceful unification." The declaration notes that proposals put forward by both sides for reunification "have elements in common." The final sentence of the joint declaration states that President Kim invited his North Korean counterpart to visit Seoul, and Kim Jong Il "agreed to visit . . . at an appropriate time in the future."

All five of the most recent joint New Year's Day editorials stress the continued significance of the "June 15 North-South Joint Declaration." The January 2005 editorial states: "This year is a significant year which marks the 5th anniversaries of the historic Pyongyang meeting [between Kim Dae Jung and Kim Jong Il]." The editorial gives the slogan for the year: "Let's advance holding high the flag of cooperation for national independence, cooperation for peace . . . and cooperation for reunification and patriotism!" It further opines: "It is unbearable shame on the nation that the sovereignty has been infringed upon for more than 100 years in . . . half of the country due to the 60-year-long presence of . . . U.S. troops in the wake of the Japanese imperialists' colonial rule that lasted for over 100 years."

The main barrier to unification is routinely identified as the United States. According to the 2003 editorial: "It can be said that there exists on the Korean Peninsula at present only confrontation between the Koreans in the north and south and the United States." The editorial urges Washington to ". . . stop its provocative military pressure and withdraw their aggression forces from South Korea without delay." According to the 2005 editorial: "All Koreans should stage a powerful struggle for peace against war in order to drive the U.S. troops out of South Korea, remove the very source of nuclear war, and defend the peace and security on the Korean Peninsula."

An analysis of North Korean ideology and rhetoric doesn't give a clear indication of which package (#1, #2, or #3) would be selected. One point does seem very clear: an unrelenting focus on maintaining a robust conventional national defense capability and building a nuclear capacity.

Policy.

Examining past and present policies reveals consistent national priorities of focusing on maintaining military power, centrally planned economic development, and initiatives promoting national unification. At the same time North Korea has depended for decades on substantial external assistance in the form of food, fuel, and technology to compensate for the serious inadequacies of its Stalinist economy.

General Situation. The history of Pyongyang's policies reflects the guerrilla origins of the regime. This experience has produced a record of policies that are extremely ambitious, do not deviate even in the face of great adversity, and approach domestic affairs and statecraft as perpetual warfare to be overcome through military-style campaigns.[57] This guerrilla experience also underscores the militant nature of the regime—the "military first" policy. Conceiving of policy implementation as constant struggle and preoccupied with threats—old, potential, and newly emerging (both internal and external)—leads Pyongyang to adopt a siege mentality. In its diplomatic relations, North Korea has tended to be rather hostile or belligerent. This has changed since the collapse of the Soviet bloc, and is especially evident in the past 5 years or so, as Pyongyang made efforts to be far more conciliatory and reached out to Seoul, Washington, Tokyo, and other capitals.

Security. As noted above, defense has long been Pyongyang's highest national priority. The priority has only seemed to increase over time. Particularly since the 1960s, when North Korea's relations with both the Soviets and Chinese soured, Pyongyang undertook a massive defense build up, increasing its defense production output and substantially expanding the number of uniformed personnel.

North Korea has also long been obsessed with nuclear, biological, and chemical weapons. These subjects will be dealt with in greater detail in a subsequent monograph. For the purposes of this analysis, it is important to note that research and development in these areas have been ongoing for a considerable period. This should be neither surprising nor shocking, since Pyongyang believes it has been the victim of both actual use of WMD during the Korean War and constant subjection to nuclear blackmail for decades.[58] North Korea has had a nuclear program since the 1950s, although reportedly efforts at weaponization did not get underway until the late 1970s.[59] North Korea has also had a vigorous cruise and ballistic missile program for decades, producing both for deployment at home and sale abroad. Evidence strongly suggests that Pyongyang also has exported nuclear technology and material, with the primary impetus being entrepreneurial. Most recently, in February 2005 there were claims that North Korea provided processed uranium to Libya.[60]

Economy. North Korea has a long history of heavy-handed central control of the economy. Since 1954 Pyongyang has pursued economic development through multiyear state plans—of 3, 5, 6, and 7-year durations.[61] This policy proclivity has eased only slightly in recent years and is unlikely to undergo dramatic reform any time soon. While the constitution was amended in 1998 to allow for consideration of "profit" and the establishment of "special economic zones," remarkably little actual policy follow through has occurred. One example is that, while a law on foreign investment was passed in 1984, for over a decade there was very little actual foreign investment or even serious attempts to attract foreign investment. Still, in recent years Pyongyang has stepped up efforts to attract foreign investment and capital in special zones but with modest and disappointing results. The first attempt was the Rajin-Sonbong Zone in the northeast of the country in the Tumen River border region.[62] The second effort was the establishment of a foreign investment zone at Kaesong on the western edge of the DMZ, and the third effort was the Mount Kumgang Tourist venture located east of Pyongyang near the eastern end of the DMZ. Neither investment zone has attracted the volume of investment hoped for, but at least the latter has had limited success, while the former appears to be languishing.[63] However, the Mount Kumgang tourist project has been the most lucrative of all. Under the terms of the agreement, Hyundai guaranteed North Korea US$940 million in exchange for permitting South Korean tourists to visit the scenic mountain. Since 1998 hundreds of thousands of tourists have visited the locale.[64]

Domestic economic reforms have been jerky and uncoordinated, with limited and sometimes contradictory results. In recent years the authorities have permitted farmers' markets to operate, and in July

2002 released price controls on food. These policies have appeared to make food more available, but freeing prices has caused serious inflation. While salaries were increased also, they do not seem to have kept pace with the food costs. Serious reform of the way agriculture is organized and planned does not appear to have occurred. As a result, there has been no dramatic improvement in the food situation in the country. Most recently, in January 2005, Pyongyang announced that the cereal allocation per person had been reduced by 50 grams to 250 grams—half of the minimum daily amount recommended by the World Food Program.[65]

In fact, rather than pursuing structural reforms in agriculture (or industry for that matter), North Korea's policy preference seems to be to continue to rely on foreign aid to alleviate food shortages and keep famine at bay. Foreign governments, including the United States, China, and South Korea, provide such humanitarian assistance. In early 2005, for example, Pyongyang asked Seoul for half a million tons of chemical fertilizer—the largest amount it had ever requested.[66] This is a continuation of an ongoing policy to survive economically, whereby Pyongyang has received aid from governments and nongovernment organizations. This aid-seeking policy spills over into North Korea's foreign relations, where Pyongyang exacts payments for coming to the diplomatic table. North Korea agreed to host the 2000 Inter-Korea summit after receiving at least US$500 million for its troubles.[67] Similarly, Pyongyang appears to have been promised significant amounts of Chinese assistance as incentive for sending a delegation to the Six Party Talks in Beijing.[68]

Other entrepreneurial efforts aimed at earning foreign currency include what are widely considered to be activities more befitting organized crime than a government: smuggling, narco-trafficking, counterfeiting, and gambling.[69]

Unification. Policy strands of both peaceful consensual confederation AND coercive unification are evident. Formal efforts by Pyongyang to pursue confederation go back at least to the joint declaration signed by representatives of the North and South in 1972. North Korea repeatedly has stated this policy and regularly refers to this agreement. Can this policy initiative be taken at face value? The answer apparently is no. We have learned this from the transcript of a discussion held in July 1972 between DPRK Ambassador to the German Democratic Republic (GDR) Lee Chang Su and GDR officials. According to documents discovered in the archives of the now defunct East German regime, Lee told East German leaders that the declaration was actually a tactical ploy.[70]

This ruse is consistent with other information we know about North Korean diplomatic initiatives. Admiral C. Turner Joy, chief negotiator for the United Nations (UN) Command at the truce talks at Panmunjom, noted the efforts of Pyongyang officials to use every ruse possible to promote their overarching goals. Negotiating, in short, is not seen as a substitute for military options, but rather another arena of battle.[71]

Advocating confederation did not preclude North Korea from pursuing nearly simultaneous violent and subversive efforts against South Korea. These initiatives include assassination attempts against the ROK's most senior leaders in the 1960s, 1970s, and 1980s; elaborate tunnels dug under the DMZ; and acts of terrorism. North Korean special forces infiltrated Seoul and came close to penetrating the Blue House (the residence of South Korea's president) perimeter in January 1968 before they were detected and defeated. In August 1974 another attempt to assassinate President Park Chung Hee failed, but the would-be assassin did kill South Korea's first lady. In October 1983, a bombing in Rangoon, Burma, killed 17 South Korean government officials, including 4 cabinet ministers. But perhaps the most horrifying act of terrorism carried out by North Korea was the bombing of Korean Air Lines Flight 858 in November 1987 that killed all 115 passengers and crew on board. The infiltration of special operations forces into South Korea continued into the 1990s, as the discovery of North Korean submarines and commandos attest.

As noted earlier, Pyongyang's more recent high profile claim to be pursuing a policy of peaceful unification was made at the 2000 Inter-Korean summit. The summit and related North Korean diplomatic charm offensive reflect that Pyongyang has become savvier and more adept at utilizing diplomacy over the decades. Since the early 1990s, North Korea has engaged in unprecedented waves of diplomatic activity: establishing diplomatic relations with a cluster of states, joining the UN, and participating in a variety of multilateral fora, including the Six Party Talks with South Korea, China, Russia, Japan, and the United States in Beijing. However, in

February 2005, Pyongyang announced that it was suspending its participation in the Beijing talks indefinitely.

An analysis of North Korean policies reveals efforts at piecemeal economic reform, continued preoccupation with military matters, and greater initiatives to engage with Seoul and other capitals.

Planning.

What evidence is there of preparation and coordination by the regime for the future? The data to be examined include what senior leaders say both in formal statements and in discussions with foreign officials and reporters. Revisions or additions made in major documents, such as the constitution, and new laws passed can also be important indicators. Moreover, foreign study tours and training programs conducted overseas for regime officials provide useful evidence of planning.

General Situation. In terms of aspirational policies, what is the regime thinking? If one is to go by the words of Kim Jong Il, Pyongyang is not interested in wholesale opening to the outside world and thoroughgoing reforms. According to Secretary of State Madeleine Albright, who visited North Korea in November 2000, Kim is rather cautious on this front. When Albright asked him about economic opening, he responded: "What do you mean by 'opening'? We will have to define the term first, because opening means different things to different countries. We do not accept the Western version of opening. Opening should not harm our traditions."[72]

Which countries does the regime look to as models? In terms of the number of foreign study tours and volume of personnel dispatched in recent years, China is by far above the rest. Yet, if one is to go by the words of Kim, Pyongyang is not interested in imitating the Chinese model of combining free markets and socialism. According to Albright, Kim is far more enthusiatic about Swedish socialism and Thailand's experience. "Thailand," Kim noted approvingly, "maintains a strong traditional royal system and has preserved its independence through a long turbulent history and yet has a market economy."[73]

Security. No tangible evidence beyond rhetoric suggests North Korea's willingness to give up its nuclear capability. Nor is there any evident willingness to downsize the massive military. The KPA continues to maintain cordial, if rather superficial and symbolic, relations with the militaries of China, Russia, Vietnam, and Cuba. North Korean officers continue to take specially tailored short courses at Chinese institutions of professional military education but are isolated from Chinese and other foreign students.[74]

Economics. Economics is the one major area under review where considerable evidence suggests that North Korea is actively contemplating experimentation and innovation. Nevertheless, there is no evidence of plans for radical reform of the central planning system. The highest levels seem reluctant to make such a dramatic break. The regime fears it will lose control. This concern is probably strongest among the economic planning bureaucracy which fears that major steps in this direction would threaten its own power and influence.

Ongoing foreign study tours and training programs for officials provide perhaps the best indicators that the regime is seriously contemplating significant changes in economic policy. According to Kang, in 2001 alone "more than 480 [officials] visited China, Australia, Italy, and Sweden."[75] Field trips of note since then have included China, Vietnam, and Russia, and training programs on economic related subjects for DPRK personnel at universities in China, Australia, and the United States.[76]

Other evidence consists of efforts to open new special economic zones. In 2002 North Korea sought to establish a new zone at Sinuiju on the northwest border with China. In an unprecedented move, Pyongyang appointed a Dutch-Chinese entrepreneur, Yang Bin, to direct the zone. Little indicates that the initiative was well-conceived or planned. Soon after, Yang was arrested in China, charged with various crimes, and sentenced to 18 years in prison.[77] The zone has since failed to make significant progress.

Further evidence suggests that North Korea's leaders are very keen on pursuing high tech projects, especially in the field of information technology (IT). Pyongyang apparently has a small but vigorous IT sector. In the late 1990s, it reportedly developed an award winning computer game, and in 2002 embarked on its first Internet joint venture with a South Korean firm.[78] These are very small steps, and nothing indicates that Pyongyang is preparing to overcome the major impediments to pursuing IT.

Unification. On unification, there is no sense of urgency, let alone any indication of planning—e.g., detailed proposals—by Pyongyang to move on the nuts and bolts of unification or confederation. At the very least, one might expect some discussion of or proposals for Kim Jong Il to visit Seoul in the near future to make good on the joint statement that he and Kim Dae Jung issued in June 2000. Thus far, there has been none. While some hyping of road and rail links across the DMZ has occurred, none have been completed, much less becoming operational.[79]

An examination of the key indicators of North Korean planning suggests that the regime continues to think about and prepare for the future. While there is little evidence that new thinking pervades Pyongyang's approach to security or unification matters, significant indications suggest that North Korea is contemplating further economic reforms. However, what is under consideration appears far removed from systemic transformation and opening.

CONCLUSIONS

Which package of intentions is Pyongyang pursuing? It remains difficult to say with certainty. Nevertheless, the above analyses provide considerable insight and strong hints.

Modest Security: Wishful Thinking?

A careful analysis of propaganda, policy, and planning leads to a high degree of skepticism about the possibility that North Korea is focused on mere survival: simply maintaining a self-defense capability, engineering a modest economic recovery, and coexisting peacefully with South Korea. Pyongyang appears to have far more ambitious intentions, and nothing indicates absolute desperation on the part of North Korean leaders. As David Kang notes: the leaders of "countries [that are] falling to pieces do not engage in long-term planning."[80] The indications are that Pyongyang envisions a bright future—significant economic changes are under consideration, and foreign models are being examined.

Ambitious Benevolence: Cautious Optimism?

A careful analysis of propaganda makes it a conceivable possibility that Pyongyang's intentions are focused in the direction of arms control, a policy of economic reform and opening, and pursuing some form of peaceful confederation with Seoul. Pyongyang propaganda insists that North Korea seeks a peaceful negotiated settlement of the nuclear issue and is committed to the denuclearization of the peninsula.[81] However, actual Pyongyang policies and planning do not seem to bear this out. When one remembers that the most consistent strand of North Korea's propaganda continues to be the essential need for military strength and the "military first" policy, then a healthy dose of skepticism emerges. Moreover, evidence from planning is unclear, so overall the data remain inconclusive.

Ambitious Malevolence: Reluctant Pessimism.

There is a real possibility that North Korea's key strategic goals are to build up its WMD programs, engage in parasitic extortionism, and pursue unification by force or coercion. According to Pyongyang's propaganda, maintaining its military strength is the regime's foremost priority. This is born out by examinations of implemented policy, planning, and ruminations about the future. As for the economy, while propaganda has made vague claims about redoubling efforts to improve economic performance, very limited evidence suggests policies of thoroughgoing reform. North Korea's history of central planning and the absence of any obvious blue print for how to proceed suggest that systemic reform is unlikely. Pyongyang appears likely to continue to hope that ad hoc changes, coupled with continued foreign aid and income generated from arms sales, tourism, and criminal activity, will be adequate to meet the country's needs. As for unification, propaganda, although it stresses using peaceful means to unification, also urges a united front between North and South Korea against the United States. Statements continue to call for the withdrawal of U.S. forces from South Korea. An examination of the record of unification policy suggests that Pyongyang believes that South Korea's government enjoys no real popular support and is merely a U.S. puppet. With the United States out of the picture, North Korea thinks it could relatively easily bring about the collapse of the South Korean regime and unification under the auspices of Pyongyang through limited military acts. North Korea has yet to put forward a clear blue print for peaceful unification and then follow through on it.

In the final analysis, there are insufficient data to say with absolute certainty what North Korea's strategic intentions are. Any one of these three "packages" outlined is plausible, or intentions could conceivably fluctuate among the three, depending on how the regime assesses the situation at any particular point. We need to probe and prod the Pyongyang regime to learn for sure. We need to keep an open mind and continually monitor what North Korea says, does, and prepares for. We should look for consistencies and inconsistencies. While not entirely discounting propaganda, we should pay closest attention to what the regime is actually doing and planning for, and give less credence to what it says. We do not want to reward and reinforce bad behavior, but at the same time it is important to provide incentives for good behavior. Complete, verifiable, and irreversible dismantlement (CVID) of North Korea's nuclear program is a laudable goal. However, the level of mutual distrust and suspicion is such that some intermediate confidence-building measures are necessary to develop trust on both sides.

ENDNOTES

1. President George W. Bush is quoted as saying, "I loathe Kim Jong Il!" See Bob Woodward, *Bush at War*, New York: Simon and Schuster, 2002, p. 340.

2. See the discussion in Marcus Noland, *Famine in North Korea: Causes and Cures*, Working Paper 99-2, Washington, DC: International Institute for Economics, 1999. For two studies, see Andrew Natsios, *The Great North Korean Famine: Famine, Politics, and Foreign Policy*, Washington, DC: United States Institute of Peace, 2001; Meridith Woo-Cumings, *The Political Ecology of Famine: The North Korean Catastrophe and Its Lessons*, Tokyo: Asian Development Bank, 2001.

3. There are considerable differences of opinion about the nature of the power structure and policy process in North Korea. Most analysts view the regime as totalitarian, but some scholars, including Selig Harrison, appear ambivalent about that, referring to the system variously as "totalitarian" and "corporatist." Selig Harrison, *Korean Endgame*, Princeton University Press, 2001. A detailed analysis of the North Korean political system will be the focus of a second monograph to be published by SSI later this year.

4. This manuscript has benefited from careful readings by some very knowledgeable people, including Guy Arrigoni, Don Boose, Ralph Hassig, Jiyul Kim, Katy Oh, and Dwight Raymond. It should be noted these individuals do not necessarily agree with all of the analysis or findings presented herein. Moreover, any errors or leaps are logic are solely the responsibility of the author.

5. However, the list of experts should not be considered exhaustive and does not include everyone researching and writing on North Korea. Moreover the sample does not include specialists primarily focused on the North Korean economy (e.g., Nicholas Eberstadt), military (e.g., Joseph Bermudez), foreign relations (Samuel Kim), or history (Charles Armstrong).

6. All the analysts listed in the text appear hold both the former and the latter views. The distaste for the repressive Pyongyang regime is also evident in the writings from analysts often considered sympathetic to the North Korea system. Bruce Cumings, for example, calls the regime an "abhorrent family dictatorship" and places blame for the "truly inexcusable . . . suffering of the North Korea people" squarely on its shoulders. See Bruce Cumings, *North Korea: Another Country*, New York: The New Press, 2004, pp. 207, 189. David Kang says "the regime's actions are abhorrent and morally indefensible." See Victor Cha and David Kang, *Nuclear North Korea: A Debate About Engagement Strategies*, New York: Columbia University, 2003, p. 46.

7. Harrison, *Korean Endgame*, p. 25.

8. These quotes come from *Ibid.*, pp. xxi, 6, and 26, respectively.

9. *Ibid.*, pp. 139-140.

10. *Ibid.*, pp 75-78.

11. *Ibid.*, p. xxi.

12. David Kang, "North Korea: Deterrence Through Danger," in Muthiah Alagappa, ed., *Asian Security Practice: Material and Ideational Influences*, Stanford, CA: Stanford University Press, 1998, p. 263.

13. Kang in Victor Cha and David Kang, *Nuclear North Korea*, p. 43.

14. *Ibid.*, p. 119.

15. Kang, "North Korea," p. 240.

16. Kang in Cha and Kang, *Nuclear North Korea*, p. 114.

17. Kang, "North Korea," p. 236.

18. Cumings, *North Korea*, p. 184.

19. *Ibid.*, pp. 1, 151.

20. Cumings quotes with apparent approval the conclusions of Anthony Namkung. *Ibid.*, p. 61.

21. Cha in Cha and Kang, *Nuclear North Korea*, p. 21.

22. *Ibid.*, p. 18.

23. Kongdan Oh and Ralph C. Hassig, *North Korea Through the Looking Glass*, Washington, DC: The Brookings Institution, 2000, p. 63.

24. *Ibid.*, p. 192.

25. *Ibid.*, pp. 110-111.

26. Stephen Bradner, "North Korea's Strategy," in Henry D. Sokoloski, ed., *Planning for a Peaceful Korea*, Carlisle Barracks, PA: U.S. Army War College, Strategic Studies Institute, 2001, p. 40.

27. *Ibid.*, p. 39.

28. *Ibid.*, pp. 28-30.

29. *Ibid.*, pp. 32-38

30. *Ibid.*, p. 37.

31. *Ibid.*, p. 28.

32. Cha and Kang, *Nuclear North Korea*, p. 4.

33. *Ibid.*, p. 110.

34. Kim Il Sung biographer Dae-suk Suh writes that "at times [North Korea seems to adopt a] completely irrational attitude toward others." *Kim Il Sung: The North Korean Leader*, second edition with a new preface, New York: Columbia University Press, 1995, p. 305.

35. Kang in Cha and Kang, *Nuclear North Korea*, p. 67; Cha in *ibid.*, pp. 84-85. The former highlights Pyongyang's alarm, while the latter downplays it.

36. *Ibid.*, p. 54. Kang argues that deterrence has worked both in preventing a North Korean attack against South Korea and vice versa.

37. Cha in Cha and Kang, *Nuclear North Korea*, p. 85; Harrison, *Korean Endgame*, p. 64; Oh and Hassig, *North Korea*, p. 77.

38. Bradner, "North Korea's Strategy," p. 33.

39. Cha in Cha and Kang, *Nuclear North Korea*, pp. 18, 21.

40. Herbert Simon is credited with the concept. The term is explicitly discussed by at least one set of analysts under review. See Oh and Hassig, *North Korea*, p. 192.

41. Cha in Cha and Kang, *Nuclear North Korea*, p. 21.

42. The quotes are from Kang in Cha and Kang, *Nuclear North Korea*, pp. 102, 103, 104.

43. *Ibid.*, p. 104.

44. Madeleine Albright with Bill Woodward, *Madam Secretary*, New York: Miramax Books, 2003, p. 467.

45. Bradner, "North Korea's Strategy"; Charles K. Armstrong, "Inter-Korean Relations: A North Korean Perspective," in Samuel S. Kim, ed., *Inter-Korean Relations: Problems and Prospects*, New York: Palgrave MacMillan, 2004, pp. 38-56.

46. Suh, *Kim Il Sung*, p. 305.

47. *Ibid.*, p. 305.

48. *Ibid.*, p. 304.

49. Nicholas Eberstadt, *The End of North Korea*, Washington, DC: American Enterprise Institute, 1999, p. 19, and chapter 5.

50. Suh, *Kim Il Sung*, p. 313.

51. *Ibid.*, p. 302.

52. See for example, Armstrong, "Inter-Korean Relations," p. 46.

53. See August 1947 speech quoted by Bruce Cumings, "The Corporate State in North Korea," in Hagen Koo, ed., *State and Society in Contemporary Korea*, Ithaca, NY: Cornell University Press, 1993, p. 215.

54. Inter-University Associates, Inc., "Introductory and Comparative Notes," in *Democratic People's Republic of Korea*, Gisbert H. Flanz, ed., *Constitutions of the Countries of the World*, Vol. X: Release 99-7 Issued November 1999, Dobbs Ferry, NY: Oceana Publications Inc., 1999, p. v.

55. The New Year's joint editorials were accessed in the archives of Pyongyang's Korean Central News Agency located at *www.kcna.co.jp*. The 2005 editorial is at *www.kcna.co.jp/item/2005/20050*. The editorial for 2004 can be found at *www.kcna.co.jp/item/2004/200401/news01/01.htm*; the 2003 at *www.kcna.co.jp/item/2003/200301/news01/01.htm*; a summary of the 2002 editorial is available at *www.kcna.co.jp/item/2002/200201/news01/01.htm*, while the full text was accessed via the *Foreign Broadcast Information System* (FBIS), and the 2001 at *www.kcna.co.jp/item/2001200101/news01/01.htm*.

56. Democratic People's Republic of Korea Foreign Ministry Statement (in Korean) carried by *Pyongyang Central Broadcasting Station*, February 10, 2005 and translated by FBIS.

57. Adrian Buzo, *Guerilla Dynasty: Politics and Leadership in North Korea*, Boulder, CO: Westview Press, 1999.

58. For example, North Korea appears convinced that the United States used biological weapons in the Korean War. Although Washington certainly considered the use of such weapons, all the evidence to date indicates that it refrained from doing so. Nevertheless, the belief that the United States did remains strong. The belief is perpetuated by slap dash Western scholars who assert myth as fact. See, for example, Harrison, *Korean Endgame*, pp. 9-10. For a noble effort to set the record straight, see Conrad C. Crane, "Chemical and Biological Warfare During the Korean War: Rhetoric and Reality," *Asian Perspective*, Vol. 25, No. 3, 2001, pp. 61-84.

59. Alexandre Y. Mansurov, "The Origins, Evolution, and Current Politics of the North Korean Nuclear Program," *The Nonproliferation Review*, Vol. 2, No. 23, Spring-Summer 1995, pp. 25-26.

60. David E. Sanger and William J. Broad, "Test Said to Tie Deal on Uranium to North Korea," *New York Times*, February 2, 2005; Glenn Kessler, "North Korea may Have Sent Libya Nuclear Material, US Tells Allies," *Washington Post*, February 2,

2005; David E. Sanger and William J. Broad, "Using Clues from Libya To Study a Nuclear Mystery," *New York Times*, March 13, 2005.

61. For a list of these plans and their basic emphases, see Noland, *Avoiding the Apocalypse*, pp. 66-67, Table 3-1.

62. *Ibid.*, pp. 133-139.

63. On the Rajin Sonbong Zone, see Oh and Hassig, *North Korea*, p. 64. On the Kaesong Zone, see Norimitsu Onishi, "2 Koreas Forge Economic Ties to Ease Tensions," *New York Times*, February 8, 2005.

64. Oh and Hassig, *North Korea*, p. 181; and Noland, *Avoiding the Apocalypse*, pp. 139-140.

65. "North Korea Slashes Food Rations" British Broadcasting Corporation report, January 24, 2005, accessed at *http://news.bbc.co.uk/1/hi/world/asia-pacific/4200861.stm* on March 1, 2005.

66. "N. Korea Asks for a Record Amount of Fertilizer," *Chosun Ilbo*, February 6, 2005, accessed on *http://English.chosun.com/w21data/html/news/200502/200502060017/html* on March 1, 2005.

67. Gordon Fairclough, "South Korean Officials Paid North Before 2000 Summit, Panel Says," *Wall Street Journal*, June 26, 2003.

68. On speculation, see, for example, Mark Magnier, "'Unofficial Visit' Includes Pledge of Patience, Peking Duck and a Tour," *Los Angeles Times*, April 22, 2004.

69. See, for example, Bradner, "North Korea's Strategy," p. 24; and Noland, *Avoiding the Apocalypse*, pp. 119-121. Gambling comes from a casino operated by a Hong Kong company in the Ranjin Sonbong Zone and from the pachinko industry in Japan operated by ethnic Koreans who remit earnings to North Korea. The casino is reportedly being closed down because of Chinese pressure. See Michael Rank, "China cashes N. Korean casino chips," *AsiaTimes*, February 24, 2005, cited at *http//:www.AsiaTimes.com*, accessed on March 1, 2005.

70. The DPRK ambassador called the joint statement a "tactical measure." Cited in Bernd Schafer, "Weathering the Sino-Soviet Conflict: The GDR and North Korea, 1949-1989," *Cold War History Project Bulletin*, Issue 14/15, Winter 2003/Spring 2004, p. 32. This comment is also cited by Cha in Cha and Kang, *Nuclear North Korea*, p. 84.

71. See, for example, C. Turner Joy, with a foreword by Matthew B. Ridgeway, *How Communists Negotiate*, New York: Macmillan, 1955.

72. Madeleine Albright with Bill Woodward, *Madam Secretary*, New York: Miramax Books, 2003, p. 466.

73. *Ibid.*, p. 466.

74. Author's conversations with civilian and military analysts in China in May 2002, September 2003, and June 2004.

75. Kang in Cha and Kang, *Nuclear North Korea*, p. 110.

76. Author conversations with analysts in China and Vietnam in November 2004; Kang in Cha and Kang, *Nuclear North Korea*, p. 116.

77. Andrew Scobell, *China and North Korea: From Comrades-in-Arms to Allies at Arm's Length*, Carlisle Barracks, PA: U.S. Army War, College Strategic Studies Institute, March 2004, p. 8.

78. Nina Hachigan, "The Internet and Power in One-Party Asian States," *Washington Quarterly*, No. 25, Summer 2002, pp. 44-45; Sonni Efron, "Computer Chips Stacked to Master Japanese Chess,"*Los Angeles Times*, August 19, 1999; and "North Korean Launches High-Tech Venture," *ibid.*, April 1, 2002.

79. See, for example, "Seoul to Finish S-N Railroad by December," *Korea Times*, February 24, 2005.

80. Kang in Cha and Kang, *Nuclear North Korea*, p. 116.

81. North Korean Foreign Ministry statement of February 10, 2005.